FAITH
ON THE
LINE

Charles Colson

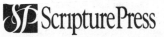 Scripture Press

Raans Road, Amersham-on-the-Hill, Bucks HP6 6JQ, England

© Scripture Press Foundation (UK) Ltd,
First published in the USA 1986 by Victor Books a division
of Scripture Press Publications, Inc, Wheaton, Illinois, USA

First British edition 1994

ISBN 1 872059 96 1

Production and Printing in England for
SCRIPTURE PRESS FOUNDATION (UK) LTD
Raans Road, Amersham-on-the-Hill, Bucks HP6 6JQ by
Nuprint Ltd, Station Road, Harpenden, Herts AL5 4SE.

CONTENTS

Publisher's Note

Chuck Colson's prophetic call
to the church and her people is
by no means new. Much of this material
appeared in his earlier four-book
"Challenging the Church" series
published by Victor Books.

Believing the timeliness and
timelessness of Chuck's message,
we now offer this updated,
one-volume edition, with the hope that you
will be freshly challenged
to put your faith on the line.

INTRODUCTION

Faith on the Line was previously published as a series of small books taken from speeches I delivered in the early 1980s, in which I called Christians to a righteous, holy life unconformed to the culture. Looking back, evangelicals were living in relative ease. A few years earlier, *Newsweek* had declared "the year of the evangelical."

But in the mid-1980s came scandals involving several prominent evangelical leaders. In the 1988 presidential election the public viewed evangelicals and the religious right as just another special interest group. And as the 1990s dawned, a Gallup poll found that evangelicals are among the most feared people in America.

Today, a "culture war" rages in our nation: the struggle between two conflicting worldviews. On one side are those who cleave to a Judeo-Christian understanding of absolute truth, with a corresponding view of life and culture based on two central commandments — love for God and love for people. On the other side are those who believe truth can be defined by each individual, with a corresponding view of life and culture based on individual choice — "what's right for me."

The culture war escalates with each passing day, as those two diametrically opposed perspectives face off on issues like abortion, the militant homosexual agenda, the cause and cure for crime, medical ethics, education, and economics.

Never before has the need been more urgent for Christians to bring their faith to the front lines. Christians must be equipped to articulate a Christian apologetic on the issues. It takes courage to think and act Christianly in times like these.

But in any age Christians are called to declare the truth through holy living and an unashamed declaration of the truth. We must demonstrate Christian love and compassion to even those who oppose us most vehemently. And so the message of those speeches I delivered a decade ago is as relevant as ever, even though in some places it was updated to fit today's cultural context.

If you're familiar with my other books, this one will serve as a refreshing reminder of familiar themes; if you're new to my writing, this book will be a good introduction. In either case, as you read the pages that follow, I pray God will use them for His purposes in your life — and that you might put your faith on the line each day, for His glory in the course of the battle for the hearts and minds of our culture.

Charles W. Colson
August 11, 1993

CHAPTER ONE

Presenting Belief in an Age of Unbelief

For more than thirty years each technological advance and expansion of government power was measured against the vision of George Orwell's extraordinary novel *1984*.

Now, in retrospect, the judgment of most commentators has been nearly unanimous: Orwell, sick and disillusioned with the vain promise of Socialist utopia, was overly pessimistic. He underestimated the strength of the West economically and politically, failed to reckon with the human spirit, and as a struggling agnostic, could not anticipate the work of a sovereign God in history. There has been no "Big Brother" or "Newspeak" (at least not in the obvious form Orwell pictured), no telescreens or thought control. We have escaped those dire predictions — so far. But have we really?

There is, I believe, a profound insight buried in Orwell's exaggerated satire. It is captured in this reflection of Winston Smith's: "It struck him [Orwell] that the truly characteristic thing about modern life was not its cruelty and insecurity but simply its barrenness, its dinginess, its listlessness." Smith continues, saying that in such a milieu, "Orthodoxy means not thinking, not needing to think; orthodoxy is unconsciousness."

The Sin of Our Times

If we are honest, it would be difficult to find a more accurate characterization of our times. And if we are honest, we are forced to admit that what only a tyrannical Big Brother could accomplish in Orwell's *1984*, our self-indulgent Western society has very nearly managed to do to itself today. Of course, our seduction has been more subtle and therefore far more insidious—through the influences of mass media and advertising, the relentless pursuit of hedonism, and the unthinking, uncritical acceptance of prevailing and declining moral and educational values.

We have, to an alarming degree, become victims of our own mindless conformity—self-absorbed, indifferent, empty of heart, the "hollow men" that T.S. Eliot wrote about in the early part of the century. Yes, orthodoxy has become unconsciousness; nihilism is the spirit of this spiritless age.

A tragic example of this was the death of David Kennedy, the fourth son of the late Senator Robert Kennedy. Kennedy, twenty-eight, was found dead in a Palm Beach, Florida hotel room, apparently the victim of a drug overdose.

Referring to David's struggle with drugs, a friend reported to *The Washington Post*, "In David's case, there was nothing to connect to in life. Even free of the drug influence, there was a deep, overpowering sense of nihilism in his personality. No person, no job, no hobby could give him something to plug into."

Dorothy Sayers, the astute contemporary of C.S. Lewis, said the sin of our times is the sin that believes in nothing, cares for nothing, seeks to know nothing, interferes with nothing, enjoys nothing, hates nothing, finds purpose in nothing, lives for nothing, and remains alive because there is nothing for which it will die.

When researcher George Barna asked Americans if they believed there was any such thing as absolute truth, 66 percent said no. When he posed the same question to conservative evangelical Christians, 53 percent said they didn't believe in absolute truth. Barna's research also showed that 44 percent of the baby-boomers say there's no cause that would lead them to fight and die for their country. Well, without the underpinnings of *truth*, what is there — beyond *self* — to live or die for?

Totalitarianism is not the conquering tyrant, enslaving us to the state; it is nihilism. We have yielded to the insidious enslavement of self-gratification. The villain, in short, is us, even those who call themselves Christians.

Too extreme a view, you say? Consider just these few manifestations:

● In the name of the "right" of a woman to

control her own body, 28 million unborn children have been murdered in America since 1973, when abortion was legalized. Who, I might ask, has inflicted a more widespread tyranny—Hitler, a maniacal dictator, or an uncaring, indifferent society? Sure, a few "religious fanatics" rant and rave, but most people are unmoved. Orthodoxy has become unconsciousness.

● As a society, we have believed Socrates, that sin is the result of ignorance, and Hegel, that man is evolving through increasing knowledge to superior moral levels. And so we've done away with any sense of individual responsibility.

What delusions! In this, the most educated and advanced society the world has ever known, we have a 50 percent divorce rate, soaring violent-crime rates, and widespread child abuse and neglect. . . . A valueless culture breeds the most awful tyranny.

● As a nation we have been blessed with unprecedented material abundance; but what it has produced is a boredom so pervasive that drug use is epidemic. A few years back I was talking with an extremely successful businessman, a great entrepreneur whose name you

would immediately know. He told me excited-
ly that he had discovered a great untapped
potential business: drug and alcohol rehabilita-
tion. "It's the fastest growth industry in America, with surefire profits," he told me. So dramatic has been the recent increase in drug and
alcohol addiction that our facilities are completely incapable of handling the casualties.

The obsessive egocentricity of secular culture today—Scott Peck calls it "narcissism" in
his book *People of the Lie*—creates a special tyranny of its own. Like the young woman cited
in a *Psychology Today* magazine article, her
nerves shot from too many all-night parties,
her life an endless round of pot, booze, and
sex. When asked by a therapist, "Why don't
you stop?" her startled reply was, "You mean I
really don't have to do what I want to do?"

Who is the tyrant in our hedonistic society?
Not Big Brother. Us.

Francis Schaeffer used to say that modern
man has both feet planted firmly in midair.

The Church in Trouble

But the most frightening fact of our world today is that the church of Jesus Christ is in

almost as much trouble as the culture. Unthinkingly, we have almost completely bought into the counterfeit secular value system. In fact, we can one-up it, since God is on our side. Unfortunately, this skewed Gospel and cheap grace are what prevent the church from making any real impact for Christ.

Many Christians attribute our impotence to the fact that we are being overrun by the culture, victimized by the media; that the reason we can't get our message across to the secular world is because we are thwarted by those who control the all-powerful tube.

And powerful it is. A study conducted by the *Detroit Free Press* showed that adults as well as children, when cut off from TV, suffer symptoms similar to drug withdrawal. Significantly, 120 households were offered $500 each to participate in the study, giving up thirty days of television. Only 27 accepted.

Christian philosopher Soren Kierkegaard was uncannily prophetic when more than a century ago he wrote,

Suppose someone invented an instrument, a convenient little talking tube, which could be heard over the whole land. I wonder if the police would forbid it fearing that the whole country would become mentally deranged if it were used.

Those who can control the tube or other forms of media wield tremendous power. For instance, when I speak to the media about my conversion, I *always* deliberately say, "I accepted Jesus Christ"; but reporters will invariably translate that into my "religious conversion," or "conversion to Christianity," or even "born again," now that the term has been so secularized as to be harmless. How the world fears the person of Jesus Christ! Christianity? Fine. It preaches peace. But introduce a risen Lord and that arouses fierce antagonism.

One major American daily, in fact, refuses to use the word "Christ" when speaking about Jesus. To do so would be to make an editorial judgment—that Jesus was the Messiah.

But there is another side. When once I was with the president of one of the television networks, I chided him for not putting more wholesome family programming on prime-time television. And since Gallup polls show that one third of all Americans claim to be born again, I told him he was missing a good market by not airing more shows with Christian values.

"Oh," he replied, "You mean like *Chariots of Fire?*"

"Yes," I exclaimed. "I've seen it ten times. I think it's one of the most powerful penetrations of the Gospel into the arts in this generation."

"Well," he said, "CBS ran *Chariots of Fire* as its Sunday Night Movie some months ago. That same night NBC had *On Golden Pond* and ABC had *My Mother's Secret Life*—a soap opera about a mother who was hiding her past as a prostitute. Let me tell you the ratings. *On Golden Pond* was number one, with 25.2 percent of all TV sets in America tuned in. *My Mother's Secret Life* drew a rating of 25.1 percent. Way in the distance, losing its shirt was CBS with *Chariots of Fire*—11.8 percent. Of the sixty-five shows rated that week 'Dallas' was number one, *Chariots of Fire* number fifty-seven."

Then he looked at me smugly and asked, "So where, Mr. Colson, are your 50 million born-again Christians?" I had no answer. Where were we? Where are we?

You see, in *1984*—the novel, that is—the instrument by which Big Brother controlled

people was the telescreen. He saw everything;
if they looked back into the telescreen they
saw Big Brother. But when *we* look into the
television set we see something much more
terrifying than the image of Big Brother. We
see ourselves. Television is but a mirror reflection. Orthodoxy has become unconsciousness.

Alexander Solzhenitsyn, the Nobel laureate
whom I consider one of the greatest prophetic
voices of God today, captured the dilemma of
our times brilliantly in his speech accepting
the Templeton Prize for the Advancement of
Religion. He recalled during his childhood in
Russia that when great disasters came, people
would respond, "Men have forgotten God.
That's why all this has happened." And in his
survey of twentieth-century Western culture,
Solzhenitsyn could find nothing better to describe what has happened than that pithy Rus-
sian proverb, "Men have forgotten God."

The great drama of our day is deeper than
totalitarianism versus democracy or East versus
West. The real struggle is belief versus unbelief.

Is Carl Sagan's creed, which is taught in our
schools, correct — that "the Cosmos is all there
is or ever will be" — or is there a sovereign God
who manifests Himself in His Word and in the

person of Jesus Christ, the same yesterday, to-day, and forever? That's the great battle—and it's uphill.

The Challenge of Change

So the great question for us as evangelical Christians charged with making disciples of all nations, is how to fulfill our biblical commission in such a time as this, bringing meaning to a culture wallowing in meaninglessness.

How *do* we present a message of belief in an age of unbelief? Charting our course is made all the more challenging when we recognize that the very nature of evangelicalism, evangelism included, as we've known it is in a time of transition, making some dramatic changes inevitable.

Consider just these four factors of change:

The first is leadership. Over the past four decades, one man, Billy Graham, has been singularly used of God—quite possibly as the greatest evangelist of all time. I hope Billy will continue preaching for a long, long time. John Wesley did until he was eighty-seven. But we evangelicals who have relied so heavily on him must recognize that the day will come when he cannot.

That day will, I believe, also mark the end of the era of stadium mass evangelism — at least in the United States. Billy's unique charisma always generates a sense of expectancy and excitement, but for anyone else, and for almost any other purpose, with each passing year it becomes more difficult to bring thousands into stadiums. There are a host of sociological reasons: crime in urban areas, television, growing public apathy, lack of effective organization, to mention but a few.

In my opinion, when the mantle of leadership is passed, it will fall not to any one individual, but to hundreds, perhaps thousands. One of the most thrilling moments of my Christian life was to see nearly 5,000 evangelists from all over the world in Amsterdam for Billy's first conference for itinerant evangelists in 1983. It is impossible for me to describe the excitement in that auditorium. Men and women from every nation sat furiously taking notes as Billy and others shared their most intimate experiences as evangelists and coached them on how to preach, how to prepare sermons, how to discern the needs of their audience. I hope Billy will do much more of this in the years ahead, and that through this remarkable man God will continue to raise up thousands of disciples to plant the Gospel in every corner of the earth. But we must recognize that evangelism leadership will be diffused—and spread around the world.

The second is the changing nature of the media. As the extraordinary technological breakthroughs of recent years—instant communications, home satellite receivers, and the like—have dramatically changed American habits, so have they begun to change the character of the American evangelist. Modern technology permitted the remarkable growth of Christian television and created new Christian folk heroes almost overnight. So great was the hunger of the evangelical viewer to be affirmed in his own beliefs that funds poured in.

But the honeymoon was short-lived, for many reasons, one being that television, by its very nature, must provide ever-increasing thrills to hold its audience; otherwise its viewers just switch channels. And to catch the attention of viewers used to thirty-second commercials, it has to reduce the Gospel message to simple slogans.

As the novelty of Christian TV wore off, a winnowing process began. TV evangelists tell me that even in good markets it is difficult to maintain their needed financial support. As TV evangelists are "forced" to plead for funds to remain on the air, airtime for the real message grows less and less.

I hasten to add, however, that quality programming with theological integrity will prosper. Witness the incredible growth of Jim Dobson's outstanding radio series, just to mention one of many examples.

Third, the great charismatic explosion, which began several decades ago, may be tapering off. Traditional evangelicals, by the way, owe much to the charismatic movement for bringing back to the church a sense of the supernatural, of worship, of adoration. But like all movements that begin with great spontaneity, this too is becoming institutionalized and large numbers of charismatics are settling into the mainstream of the church.

Fourth, the process of "privatization," as Os Guinness calls it, sadly will intensify as society becomes more impersonal and individuals feel more alienated. People will, I fear, continue to compartmentalize their lives including their religious experience. Ask a Christian layperson his ministry and he will inevitably respond, "Gideons on

Thursday night," or "Prison Fellowship on Monday night," or, "Sunday School." The process of privatization destroys our understanding of ministry that is twenty-four hours a day, being Christ's person wherever we are, in business, the home, the country club, or the ghetto.

Jay Kesler, president of Taylor University, says the church today is like a pro football game: 100,000 people sitting in the stands watching 22 men on the field beating themselves to a pulp. True Christianity is not a spectator sport; it is not to be sat out in church pews; it is to be lived out in the world so that "the blessings of God might show forth in every area of life" as the great Puritan pastor Cotton Mather put it.

These developments should cause us thoughtfully and prayerfully to examine our strategy for evangelism for the balance of this century. In this spirit, let me suggest five areas of challenge and opportunity.

Witness As a Way of Life

First, authentic evangelism must involve the totality of life. Jesus said, "You *shall* be My witnesses," but a lot of Christians have taken that commandment to mean that we are *to* witness. So we have reduced evangelism to verbal formulas, neat, easy-step plans; just utter these simple phrases and you'll be part of the club.

And some people seem to think that the simpler we can communicate the Gospel, the more people we can recruit. Maybe so, but the question is "recruit them for what?" Millard Fuller of Habitat for Humanity tells the story of his experience in Zaire, where Christians had trained parrots to say, "I love Jesus." Not unfairly, I think, Fuller likens many who sit in pews every Sunday morning, mindlessly chanting their creeds, to those parrots.

Packaging the Gospel into tidy packages has some serious dangers. For one thing, it tends to cheapen the message. When we tell the world that all there is to becoming a Christian is a simple prayer—and thereafter God will shower blessings upon them—we are selling the world a false bill of goods. We will pay for it—if not from the angry disillusioned millions to whom we sell our false message, then surely on Judgment Day. Then too we can easily fall into the snare of turning evangelism into a big game hunt—keeping score and measuring success by the fame and power of our convert trophies.

This is why it is so important to focus on Jesus' command that we *be* witnesses. Jesus means, I believe, that evangelism is to involve the totality of our lives. Everything about our lifestyle counts—how we spend our money, how we treat our children, our business ethics, our political values, our domestic relations, and on and on. (And this means far more than being faithful in church every Sunday morning or not smoking, drinking, using foul language, or associating with those who do.)

Christians are supposed to be humble, yet we can get caught up in our own importance and power. During a press conference at a Christian broadcasters' convention, a reporter from a prominent national daily challenged me, "I don't know what all this born-again business means, but I have been at this convention two days, and everywhere I go the people I interview seem to think they have all the answers. As a matter of fact, the bigger the exhibit, the more arrogant the individual. Aren't born-again Christians supposed to be loving?"

I defended my brethren, pointing out that

most of them enter the ministry for all the best reasons, but that we Christians are not immune to the seduction of power. But I had to bite my lip because I know exactly what that reporter was talking about—and so do you.

As we present the Gospel to an unbelieving world we need to hold before us the words of Paul: "Let this mind be in you, which was also in Christ Jesus." Though He was God, He "made Himself of no reputation, and took upon Him the form of a servant" (Philippians 2:5, 7, KJV).

When I came to Christ I realized that my great sin had been pride. But those words— "let this mind be in you"—ring in my ears constantly. God does not let me forget them and my utter dependency on Him for grace to reach out to others in His name.

How we need to be reminded of the oft-quoted adage that "evangelism is like one beggar showing another beggar where he found bread."

Joseph Bayly's book *The Gospel Blimp* should be mandatory reading for evangelicals. While we are creating sophisticated organizations and employing the latest technology to win the

world to Christ, let us not forget that our
neighbors judge Jesus Christ by what they see
in us.

Discipling Believers

Second, evangelism demands serious discipleship. Our task is not simply to get people to
recite certain prayers so we can move on to
more fertile fields. We are to help lead them
to Christ and then teach them spiritual disci-
plines and truths so that they truly can become disciples — followers of Christ, and in
time, teachers themselves. One-on-one minis-
tries like The Navigators will, I believe, become increasingly strategic in the decades
ahead.

When I asked Christ into my life, I had never heard of evangelical Christianity. I didn't
know the jargon or formulas of the evangelical
subculture. If there hadn't been someone to
take me by the hand and walk me through the
Scriptures, help me to pray, help me to feel
comfortable with others, I really wonder where
I would be today. Doug Coe discipled me constantly. Harold Hughes, my one-time political
enemy, loved me even when most people in

my own political party turned their backs on me. Al Quie, then a congressman, offered to go to prison for me. Fred Rhodes took early retirement from government to help me start Prison Fellowship. And down through the years there have been men like Carl Henry, Richard Lovelace, R.C. Sproul, Dick Halverson, and others who have given so much of themselves to teach me. Whatever growth I have experienced as a Christian has been in large measure due to the sacrificial commitment of others who were willing to invest themselves in me.

And this kind of evangelism cannot be deterred. Mass evangelism through television could be eliminated tomorrow. Funds could dry up; government policies could change; so could media ownership; we could be subjected to oppression in this country that would deny the free proclamation of the Gospel.

But there is no power than can ever stop one-on-one discipleship. Across the country Prison Fellowship has trained a band of dedicated men and women who mentor Christian prisoners facing the tough transition back to the outside world. Clair VanZeelt of Chicago demonstrates the commitment of some of these volunteers. Even before being trained—on his very first trip inside Cook County Jail—Clair met inmate Jimmy. Handing Jimmy a printed Bible study lesson, Clair said, "I'll be back next week and give you another one."

When Clair returned, Jimmy had been transferred to another, tougher facility. Though it took Clair two weeks to cut through red tape, he found Jimmy and delivered a second lesson. When Clair returned a third time, Jimmy was overwhelmed. "You're probably the best friend I've ever had," he told Clair, who was himself amazed. "I had spent maybe a total of one hour with him," Clair says. "But his family and society had rejected him. Right then I came to appreciate what it means to express love." That was thirteen years ago, and now dozens of ex-prisoners know that Clair—"Dad"—is on the other end of the phone line, standing by with a steady hand and a word of encouragement grounded in the Word of God.

It is reported that when the missionaries left China and the Communists took over, the most awful persecution of the church, then estimated at more than 1 million believers, began. Surely, after thirty years of brutal, ruthless persecution, the church would be obliterated; instead, according to many reports, there are today more than 30 million Christians in China.

Joseph Stalin once mockingly dismissed the church's influence, asking how many divisions the Pope had. What would he say now when the church has survived and proved more powerful than the political party he ruled with an iron fist?

Penetrating the Culture

Third, for effective evangelism we must penetrate the mainstream of thought in secular culture.

Since only 8 percent of secular reporters regularly attend church, it is not surprising that most fail to discern spiritual matters. Nicaragua is a clear example. The Pope stood alone on a platform to conduct mass while Sandinista officials held back the huge, friendly crowd, took over the front-row seats, and for the benefit of the grinding TV cameras, shook their fists and screamed at the Pope.

Each time they did so, the Pope lifted his crucifix over his head. A remarkable linguist, he conducted mass in the language of the Miskito Indians, thousands of whom the Sandinistas had ruthlessly murdered. Symbolically he conveyed the powerful truth: God offers grace to the people you killed. The crowd cheered, while the protestors howled with rage at the Pope's open defiance.

It was a classic confrontation, reminding me of what historian Will Durant called the greatest drama of history—when Christ met Caesar in the arena—and Christ won. For without doubt, that unforgettable night in Managua, Christ won.

But what did American newsmen on the scene report of that classic confrontation? What did they see and hear? The Pope was inept and confused, they said, speaking in a language the crowd couldn't understand. And he failed to bring peace or healing to that troubled country. He berated Marxist priests and further divided his church.

Of course he did—and deliberately. He also indicted the Sandinistas for their massacres and their politicization of the church. He held up the indestructible truth of Christ against their shouted insults. But he did not achieve overnight reform; so the media labeled as "failure" what was in reality a truly heroic moment for Christians.

Subliminally, a nuance and a word at a time, the non-Christian perspective inexorably gains ground. If C.S. Lewis were alive today he might write of Screwtape's sad fate: Alas, he is among the unemployed; things are going quite nicely without his having to lift a finger.

To invade the secular mainstream means that Christian writers and others with creative talents must compete in the secular media. We need to infiltrate the newsrooms of *The Washington Post* and the *New York Times*, of CBS, ABC, and NBC.

We need to frame the issues in a Christian worldview. Some years ago two Los Angeles doctors were accused of murder. They had removed the life support apparatus from a comatose man whose condition they diagnosed irreversible. First went the respirator; he began to breathe on his own. Then the doctors ceased intravenous feeding. Nine days later the man died — of starvation. NBC's anchorman pegged the story with the following: "The question of when to pull the plug may be about to get a thorough hearing in a Los Angeles courtroom."

When to pull the plug? What about *if?* The treatment of a dying man is full of ethical dilemmas. But are they all to be framed in terms of *when* to pull the plug? Have we already concluded that we must pull it?

The anchorman's words suggest that the decision is merely complex, not agonizing. A cost-benefit analysis, which could be done on a computer, might resolve the moral questions. Convenience and productivity and overall cost determine who lives and who dies.

This is a scenario borrowed from the pages of Alexander Solzhenitsyn's *Cancer Ward*. In the Soviet Union, in a society free from moral impediments, that is how decisions were made.

We Christians tend to hurl invectives at the "satanic enemy" and claim it's all part of a sinister conspiracy. I overreacted in the same way during my White House days when I believed the media distorted their coverage of Mr. Nixon to suit their own biases. But the fact is that secular journalists do not choose their words as part of some conscious plot to destroy Christian values. No, it's worse than that: The choice is unconscious, simply reflecting the worldview of the writer. The word "when" is what most naturally came to mind; to a Christian, the word "if" would be natural.

We need Christian influence in the media and in the arts and in music so that God's truth becomes evident in every walk of life.

In that same vein, Christian scholars and thinkers need to do battle with secular intellects. I realize that many Christians believe that reason and faith are incompatible. But that is nonsense. Augustine said, "Believe that you may understand, understand that you may believe."

Let's face it, friends, if we fail to articulate the reasoned defense of our faith, all of our witnessing, plans of salvation, and evangelistic efforts will be for naught. Secularization of Western culture is undermining the presuppositions absolutely essential for effective evangelization. In a society that has lost a common belief in moral absolutes, relativism reigns— thus the Bible is just another book and Jesus simply another superior teacher.

Abraham Kuyper was a great Dutch theologian in the early part of this century. Kuyper argued that if Christians are going to be strong enough to stand against the philosophy of secularism, they must articulate a philosophy that is just as comprehensive as secularism. Christianity must be an all-embracing system of thought that gives us a perspective from which to view every part of life: family, church, work, politics, science, art, and culture.

In short, Christianity must be a worldview: a view of the entire world, an intellectual grid through which we can interpret everything we see or read or do. God created the world, and everything in the world relates to Him.

Kuyper didn't just talk about Christianity as a worldview. He acted on it. He worked vigorously to influence public life in the Netherlands on the basis of Christian truth. He founded a Christian university, published a newspaper, wrote daily editorials, and was eventually elected prime minister. Kuyper's social and educational reforms continue to benefit Holland today.

When the Apostle Paul preached in Athens — a culture that did not know the Scriptures — he was not afraid to introduce the Gospel in terms they would understand. He quoted Greek poetry. On Mars Hill he saw a monument to "the unknown god." Seeing that they acknowledged that a deity might exist whom they didn't know, Paul jumped at the opportunity. He saw a jumping-off point from which he could proclaim the Good News of Christ. He was willing to engage the Greek mind before he presented the Gospel.

There's a clear parallel here. We no longer live in Jerusalem. Our country is an "Athens"—unfamiliar with and hostile to our God. We cannot compromise the message, but we've got to find ways to present what we believe in a way they can understand it.

Much of our Christianity today is, sadly, entertainment for the faithful. We talk in our own language to likeminded friends, and the world is content to let us put on our own show, as long as we don't bother anyone.

But we are meant to bother the world—bother it by presenting a message that convicts people of their sin, which offers an alternative to the hollowness and nihilism of secular life.

To invade the secular mainstream—on their turf—requires great creativity and boldness. It means aggressively reaching out and battling for the hearts and minds of our neighbors.

But we can do it. That's why I was so thrilled with the advertising campaign sponsored by the Arthur S. DeMoss Foundation offering *Power for Living*, a little booklet that magnificently presented the Gospel message. It was offered over secular television and in full-page ads in the *Wall Street Journal*, the

Washington Post, and other publications. More than 7 millon people responded for information about the Gospel: tens of thousands have come to Christ through that magnificent outreach.

And we can do it on a more personal level, also. Just before a governor's prayer breakfast where I was to speak, the chairman asked me not to mention the name of Jesus Christ because there were Jews in the audience. You know what to do with advice like that—and that's what I did. The first people to thank me afterward were Jewish. Don't ever water down your message for anyone.

We need to stop talking to ourselves and speak instead to the secular world. There is real hunger out there. John Wesley said the "way to a man's heart is through his mind," so we need to be giving quality Christian literature to our non-Christian neighbors. My own Christian life began because a Christian friend handed me *Mere Christianity*. Let's lead people to the real meat: the great classics by and about Augustine, Jonathan Edwards, John Calvin, Charles Spurgeon, Dietrich Bonhoeffer, C.S. Lewis or contemporaries like Francis Schaeffer, J.I. Packer, Malcolm Muggeridge, Carl Henry, and others of their caliber.

Strengthening the Role of the Church

Fourth, the role of the church in evangelism must be strengthened. We evangelicals have had a sinfully, shamefully casual disregard for that institution for which our Lord shed His own blood. He gave Himself up for the body of Christ — the church — that the church would be the presence of God in the world, that people would see the kingdom-of-God-to-come in the people of God.

In our well-intentioned zeal to win the whole world for Christ, we have tended to concentrate on grand crusades and in the process we often diminish the responsibility of the local church. This is one of the reasons that many churches have become nothing more than Sunday morning civic clubs, places where people go for their one-hour-a-week inspirational fix.

We have allowed ourselves to drift a long way from the biblical vision of the church. Listen to how Aristides described the early church to Hadrian the Roman Emperor:

They love one another, they never fail to help widows, they save orphans from those who would hurt them. If they have something they give freely to the man who has nothing. If they see a stranger they take him home, and are happy as though he were a real brother. They don't consider themselves brothers in the usual sense, but brothers instead through the Spirit, in God.

That is evangelism, when people *see* God's power lived as a new order, their values in sharp contrast to the ways of the world. That's making the "invisible kingdom visible," as John Calvin puts it.

The success of evangelism in the next decade, I am convinced, will be in direct proportion to the strength of the local church. But because we have failed to make the church all that it is supposed to be, the culture doesn't expect much from it.

When I was in New York recently, a cab driver asked me what I do for a living.

"I'm a minister," I answered, trying to explain my writing and speaking activities in a word he would understand—not that I am an ordained clergyman.

"Oho," the cabbie said. "So you're here to get money."

It wasn't a question; it was a statement: If you're a minister, *that's* what you're after. Money.

The cabbie launched into a well-worn diatribe against Christians. "A bunch of hypocrites," he said. And he clinched his case with the Jimmy Swaggart scandal.

Frankly, it was hard to respond. I had no defense. The Jimmy Swaggart case has brought disgrace on the entire evangelical world. One person falls, and we're all painted with the same brush.

To its credit, the Assemblies of God did its best to discipline Jimmy Swaggart after his first offense, when he was caught with a prostitute. The denomination ordered him to step down from the pulpit and undergo counseling.

But Swaggart refused. Even when the denomination revoked his license to preach, he continued his ministry.

And people continued to support him.

Then Swaggart dishonored the church a second time—caught with another prostitute. This time, he was even less repentant. He told his congregation, "The Lord told me it's flat none of your business."

The lesson here is this: When a believer is

disciplined by his church, *and refuses to comply,* then the scriptural principle is to cast him out of the congregation.

The policy is described in Matthew 18: If a believer rejects the discipline of the church and continues in sin, expel him. And Paul's letter to the Corinthians explains why.

The purpose is not to be mean or vengeful. It's to impress upon the sinner the seriousness of his sin, with the hope of bringing him to repentance. *And* it's to maintain the integrity of the church before a watching world.

When the Assemblies of God church disciplined Jimmy Swaggart, the rest of the Christian world should have refused to tune in to Swaggart's program anymore or send him money.

But many people chose to follow a charismatic TV preacher instead of the church. They continued to listen to Swaggart and give him financial support.

Swaggart himself is ultimately responsible for his second offense, of course. But so are the Christians who enabled him to continue in ministry after he had defied the discipline of his church. Is it any wonder the world laughs at our evangelistic efforts?

Demonstrating the Gospel

Fifth, evangelism is more than proclamation; it is demonstration. We live in an age of deep skepticism. Most surveys reveal that people do not believe what they see and hear through the media. (Perhaps we can be grateful for that.) Public respect for institutions and professions has steadily declined. Ministers do a little better in public opinion polls than politicians, but that is not saying much.

PF's *Jubilee* newsletter recently ran a story of ex-prisoner Herbie Harris. One paragraph in his story caught my attention. For eighteen months Herbie shared a prison cell with a black Muslim. In time, the man summed up Herbie in a phrase: "You're not like a lot of other Christians." Herbie took it as a compliment — though it is another sad commentary on how the world perceives us.

There are few people, at least in the Western world, who have not *heard* the Gospel message. So we have to conclude that countless millions either reject it, do not apply it to themselves, or do not regard it as relevant. There are also millions who will never cross the threshold of our churches; as many churches flee the inner cities and head for the high ground of the suburbs, they leave behind people who simply do not feel comfortable enough — or good enough — to come into our handsome sanctuaries.

How then do we break through this cultural barrier and overcome the skepticism and distrust levied toward the evangelicals? Surely that is a priority for us.

The answer lies in obedience. The gritty and sacrificial type that we sometimes, amid our comfortable and cloistered lifestyles, never even consider. But when we Christians take the biblical message to heart and have the courage to *live in obedience to Christ's radical commands,* we are compelled not only to preach the Gospel, but also to take it into the world and live it out. As Saint Francis of Assisi said, "Preach the Gospel all the time; if necessary use words."

Let me give you one example. Jefferson City is a sleepy town of 30,000 people, the capital of Missouri. It is also the site of four state penitentiaries. Most of the inmates come from Kansas City and St. Louis, several hundred miles away.

Every weekend the wives, children, and

families of inmates descend on Jefferson City to visit their loved ones in prison. Most can't afford a motel. Many have been forced to sleep in cars or parking lots or on park benches. There have been some very unfortunate incidents over the years because of the situation.

But in time, Prison Fellowship volunteers saw the needs of these unwanted visitors. They began to invite inmates' families into their homes. That became difficult to manage, however, so a small committee was formed, and an old boarding house located. Volunteers from twelve local churches raised $46,000, bought the home, and with volunteer manpower and contributions, restored it. The sparkling, renovated home officially opened in 1981. Its name? Agape House. And since November 1981 tens of thousands of guests have passed through its doors.

Any night of the week, you will find Agape House full of the wives, children, fathers, and mothers of inmates, who, for a minimal fee, get a clean bed, a Bible, and best of all, a day-care center so children can be cared for while their parents have uninterrupted time together. And one of the most exciting things about Agape House is that it is run by a former

Catholic nun and a Southern Baptist missionary.

In my book *Loving God*, I tell the story of their powerful ministry through the example of a woman I'll call Sherry.

Sherry, who knew the underside of life, worked in a bar, clinging to the thin hope that her husband, sentenced for life, would be released. One evening she was sitting at Agape House's dining room table listening to other prison widows, when the two women of God who manage Agape House came through the room, dispensing towels, asking about husbands, stopping to admire a small child's toy.

Sherry turned away from the conversation and mused, "I don't even know if there is a God. But if He is real and He is good, He must be something like these ladies at Agape House."

You see, my friends, that is not waiting for people to come into our churches or listen to our sermons on radio and television. That is taking the Gospel to them where they are, sharing in their suffering at their point of need, letting them *see* the Good News lived out through God's people.

And when we do this, the world pays attention. Not only does a hardened prisoner's wife like Sherry come to realize that there is a God, but even the secular world can see the difference we Christians make living out our faith. Agape House was even singled out by President Reagan for national recognition in 1982 — as an example to the world of what needs to be done in our communities.

The secular world sees the same thing every time our ministry conducts a community service project — when we take inmates out of prison for two weeks to help the needy, like the project that renovated the home of an elderly Atlanta widow; or the San Antonio project with Habitat for Humanity that built a house for a Spanish-speaking couple with six foster children; or the inmates in Columbia, South Carolina, who refurbished an inner-city playground just before Christmas.

Prison Fellowship is doing these projects all over the country, and each time we do, the secular media sits up and takes notice. They might not cover our church services, but they'll turn out when we invade their territory and make a difference in peoples' lives where they live. The Good News needs to be *seen* as well as heard.

A Future of Promise

What then is our challenge in the decades ahead?

How do we fulfill our biblical commission in an age of unbelief—when orthodoxy is unconsciousness?

1. By being witnesses with the totality of our lives;

2. By discipling others, one-on-one; not just making converts, but training them to live disciplined, holy lives;

3. By breaking out of our comfortable cocoons and engaging the secular world in battle for the hearts and minds of our culture;

4. By strengthening the role of the church, making it truly a holy community;

5. By taking the Gospel into a hostile, skeptical world, living it out for all to see.

An awesome challenge? Yes, indeed. But if God is for us, who can be against us? We, who know a God who is sovereign and at work in history, have no cause for timidity, but have the spirit of "power, love, and a sound mind," as the Apostle Paul wrote to Timothy (2 Timothy 1:7, KJV). We are called to be obedient to One whose will cannot be thwarted.

C.C. Goen, the eminent church historian, wrote of the Reformed tradition, "It bred a race of heroes willing to topple tyrants, carve new kingdoms out of howling wilderness, and erect holy commonwealths to fulfill the righteousness of God on Earth."

Let us be about our business, my brothers and sisters, that we might be found worthy of this, our heritage — and our sovereign Lord's mission for us.

In *Real Christianity*, written late in the eighteenth century and republished in modern English by Multnomah Press, the great Christian parliamentarian and abolitionist leader, William Wilberforce, looked at the world around him. It was a grim picture: Europe awash in tidal waves of humanism caused by the French Revolution, and in England, as Wilberforce wrote, "Infidelity has lifted up her head without shame." But he concluded:

> I must confess equally boldly that my own solid hopes for the well-being of my country depend, not so much on her navies and armies, nor on the wisdom of her rulers, nor on the spirit of her people, as on the persuasion that she still contains many who love

and obey the Gospel of Christ. I believe that their prayers may yet prevail.

There soon followed one of the great revivals of modern time. So too is it my belief that the prayers and work of those who love and obey Christ in our world may yet prevail in a revival the likes of which we've never seen.

CHAPTER TWO

The Role of the Church in Society

The role of the church in American life is being debated today as never before. And the debate has crucial consequences for those of us who call ourselves followers of Jesus Christ.

The relationship between church and state has always been a serious issue. In the first century, Christians in Rome refused to give Caesar equal billing with God. Not that they wouldn't respect Caesar; they simply wouldn't call him Lord, and for that they were thrown to the lions.

Then Emperor Constantine became a Christian and instituted the Holy Roman Empire; from then on—and for centuries afterward in Europe—nations were "Christian" nations. Church and state merged together, vying for power.

In fact, what distinguished American colonists hundreds of years later was that they were determined to provide religious freedom for every citizen. They developed a system of pluralism and, interestingly enough, it was a Christian who argued in the beginning of our nation that the state cannot convert; only the power of God can.

Distorted Pictures

My heart grieves when I read how the press talks about the church today. (I suppose the confusion is understandable: According to one survey only 8 percent of the secular press corps attend church regularly; so when they discuss spiritual issues, it's a little like calling in a team of plumbers to perform open-heart surgery.) Look at some of the religious issues misunderstood by the press:

- The first is that the church (particularly

the fundamentalist church) is going to rise up and take over America. But can you imagine the church of Jesus Christ, which can't even agree on how to interpret the Bible, having the power to take over this country? In our current fractured state, we don't have the power to take over this country. Nor do we have the disposition to do it; God provides the Spirit who will change people, not the state.

● The second nonsense that we hear today is this question of separation of church and state. The term *separation of church and state* was never even considered when the Constitution was written. It was introduced fifteen years later by Thomas Jefferson. And the separation that the founders talked about was keeping the state out of the church, not keeping the church out of the religious and moral welfare of the country. They certainly never intended that religious influence be erased from our society.

Indeed, the founding fathers based our country on Judeo-Christian beliefs and principles, and if you look through the pages of American history, what a proud tradition we Christians have. Again, Christians of the early nineteenth century were at the forefront of

founding public hospitals and public education, of meeting human needs, and stopping
abuses of working men and women. The aboli-
tion of slavery was spearheaded by Christians,
as was the civil rights movement. Don't tell
me that religion doesn't belong in public life.
You bet it does, because it's been for the moral
betterment of our country.

● The third area of confusion is the great
political debate between conservatives and liberals that threatens to polarize America and
with it the church of Jesus Christ. The conservative argument is, "Bring America back to
God and old-fashioned values." Certainly, I am
all for bringing America back to its traditional
values. But I think there is a grave danger
when we begin to talk that way, for it would
amount to creating civil religion in this land,
that is, putting the state and God on the same
basis. One recent President put it very well.
He said American government makes no sense
unless it is founded on a deeply felt religious
faith, and "I don't care what it is." You see,
that's faith in faith. It's civil religion. It's a
belief that God and country are equal. And it's
very dangerous.

On the other side of the political spectrum,

liberals say that religion is intensely personal and should have no effect on public policy. New York Governor Mario Cuomo remarked in a speech at the University of Notre Dame that, as a Christian, he believed abortion was wrong and the teaching of the church was right, but as long as a majority of the citizens of his state did not favor that position, he was not morally obligated to carry it out. In essence, Cuomo said, "God speaks truth but it has to be ratified by a majority vote of the people."

That's wrong. That kind of speech gives sophistry a bad name. Yet how did the press characterize Governor Cuomo's speech? One reporter wrote, "At last someone has cleared away all of the confusion and given us an intelligent position we can believe in." Of course, it is an intelligent position to the secular press because it denies the authority of God over our lives.

We Christians must now more than ever proclaim that Jesus Christ is Lord over all political structures. The values of the Gospel of Jesus Christ must never be held hostage to the fortune of any political party or individual.

But the issues being debated today in the press raise another question, much more fundamental than just the relationship of church and state. They raise a question about how our secular culture perceives the church. What do people really see? If you want to know something about water, the last creature you ask is a fish, because he lives in it. And if you want to know about the church, I guess the last people you really ought to ask are Christians, because we are in it and we don't really see how the world sees us.

The *Washington Post* recently featured a front-page article that characterized evangelical Christians as "largely poor, uneducated, and easy to command." If a journalist said that about any other group in America, he would be fired on the spot, but the *Post* didn't fire anyone. It merely expressed surprise that many readers found the description offensive. A few days later, one of the bemused editors explained that they felt they were simply printing something that is "universally accepted."

That illustration is a sorry example of how we evangelicals are perceived by the press.

I give three critical mistakes the world makes when it looks at the church of Jesus Christ. Are we responsible for these misguided views?

Just a Building?

The first is that when people look at the church, they tend to see a building, a physical structure—a misconception I think Christians have encouraged. How many times have you heard people say, "Let's go to church"? First-century believers didn't say, "We're going to church." They said, "We *are* the church."

The church of Jesus Christ is us! Don't speak of it as a building. Jesus never did. Jesus never said, "Come to the temple." Instead, He commanded the church, "Go! Preach the Gospel! Make disciples! Go into all the world!"

The Greek word for "church" is *ecclesia*. Not a building, not an edifice, but a gathering, an assembly of people. Actually, the first Christians were forbidden to construct buildings for worship.

Several years ago I had the opportunity to preach in the Full Gospel Church of Seoul, Korea. There were 10,000 people in the sanctuary, 15,000 in the overflow halls, six services on that Sunday. It was not the numbers that moved me; rather, I was overwhelmed by the presence of the Spirit. Afterward I told the pastor how excited I was about his church. He said, "Oh, this isn't the church; this is just where we gather Sunday morning. The church, you see, is in the home — 10,000 homes all across Seoul where members meet every morning for two hours of Bible study and prayer."

Then I understood why in that country of 35 million Buddhists and only 2 million evangelical Christians, Christian values dominate the culture. It is because Korean Christians take their faith seriously. We in this supposedly Christian nation, but one in which humanist values dominate, desperately need to learn from our Korean brothers and sisters.

The danger of thinking of the church as a building is that whenever we do, we render ourselves powerless in society.

During the 1977 energy crisis, the Commonwealth of Virginia ordered all nonessential buildings closed. Number one on the list? The church. Nonessential. All you do is open it on Sunday morning for people to come in, sit, and be entertained, and the rest of the week it sits empty. "Close the church to save energy." That's what the governor said. His fault or ours?

In Washington, D.C., one local church was

in legal "hot water" for taking in homeless people and allowing them to spend the night. The zoning authority said that that was a violation of city ordinances because the function of a church was Sunday morning worship, not giving people a place to sleep.

Slowly but surely, people are viewing the church as having a narrow, limited function, and we're lending that attitude a hand by boxing ourselves in. The great Archbishop of Canterbury William Temple (1881–1944) once said that the church of Jesus Christ is the only cooperative society that exists for the benefit of its *non*members. We're to take the church out of the walls of our sanctuaries and to the people.

Wherever a repressive regime has tried to destroy the church, it has tried to prevent Christians from reaching out to people.

In 1929, when the Soviet government wanted to wipe out the church, what did they do? They passed a law, not to close the orthodox church buildings and prohibit meetings on Sunday morning, but to make it a crime to conduct church school, to help the poor, to go into the neighborhoods and reach out to people. Believers had to stay within their churches on Sunday morning. What the Soviet Communists did *by decree* in 1929, we are allowing to be done to us today *by default*.

What a difference the church makes when we move out into society:

● When I visited the New Mexico State Penitentiary, I was excited to discover that all six men on death row were Christians who loved the Lord. The youngest, only eighteen years old, said to me, "I'm ready to die; I'm ready to be with Jesus." He continued, "But before I die I want to make a film on the problem of child sexual molestation, because I am a victim. I want to leave something that will be shown in schools to tell kids how to deal with it." The church was there in that prison because volunteers had gone in and taken the Good News to men condemned to die.

● During a Prison Fellowship seminar in a Kentucky prison, eight prisoners walked to the front of the chapel and made professions of faith in Christ. More than fifty other inmates and fifteen Prison Fellowship volunteers looked on with pride and excitement. Afterward, three inmates filled a large, galvanized horse trough in the prison yard with water, and the church gathered around it for an impromptu baptism service.

As the chaplain led each of the new Christians into the water, most wept; the eyes of their brothers in Christ and the volunteers also filled with tears. A softball game in the prison yard broke up, and the players and many others stood watching intently. A few jeered, but they were ignored. All eyes were on the eight men, who before this day had stood for nothing but wrong. Now, because of Christ, they had the courage to take a stand for Him in prison—where doing so is not only a witness, but a risk.

• Some years ago I met Jack Eckerd, the founder of Eckerd Drug Stores. We began to talk about the Christian faith, and several months later Jack Eckerd gave his life to the Lord. The first thing he did was walk into one of his 1,500 stores and see *Playboy* and *Penthouse* magazines on the bookshelves. He went back to his store managers and said, "This is wrong. We shouldn't be selling *Playboy* and *Penthouse* here. Take those magazines out of my stores."

The managers protested, "We're making a huge profit selling those magazines."

Jack Eckerd replied, "I don't care. Take those magazines out of my stores."

Now you can walk into an Eckerd Drug Store anywhere in the United States and you will find that the shelves once filled with pornography are now clean of it. As other Christians across the country voiced their protests, other chains followed suit — taking those magazines out of sight if not off the shelves completely.

● In Belfast, Northern Ireland, where the streets are torn almost daily by the bomb blasts of sectarian strife, the drama of reconciliation has taken place in the most unlikely place — the prisons. I've seen this restoration and healing firsthand. At a Prison Fellowship International conference in Belfast, we were joined by two young prisoners — Liam, a Roman Catholic, and Jimmy, a Protestant.

Liam had been the last member of the famous Maze Prison hunger strikes some years ago in which Bobby Sands led nearly a dozen fellow terrorists to their deaths. When Liam's turn came, he starved himself for fifty-five days. Blind, weak, and near death, he was visited by his mother, who convinced him to break the fast. During Liam's recovery, he realized he had to make a choice between his cause — the Irish Republican Army — and Jesus Christ.

He chose Christ—and from that point on, his faith led him to radical steps of forgiveness and love.

He began eating with his former enemies, breaking the strict segregation between Catholics and Protestants in his prison mess hall. And eventually, through Liam's witness, Jimmy, a Protestant ex-terrorist, came to know Christ. Furloughed for the week of our conference, the two stood on a stage before a huge crowd of both Catholics and Protestants. As Liam put his arm around Jimmy's shoulders, he evidenced the power of the Christ who reconciles: "Before, if I had seen Jimmy on the street," he said, "I would have shot him. Now he's my brother in Christ. I would die for him!"

● When Peru's Lurangancho Prison was known as the worst prison in the world, I visited—after a nun had been killed there and all religious workers had been barred (though Prison Fellowship volunteers were still going in). When I walked into one of the cell blocks, the smell was so putrid it was overpowering. I started to slide on the floor, and I looked down to find I was walking on sewage overflowing from each cell.

Yet at every fourth or fifth cell in that terrible place, a man would grab me by the sleeve, pull me into his cell, and with a beaming smile point to a Prison Fellowship discipleship seminar certificate hanging on the wall. A bit later, an older man grabbed my hand. He was hot and sweaty, and started to cry. He said in broken English, "You great man because you come and you love us." I wrapped my arms around him and let him cry on my shoulder. There in that awful pit of perversity and despair, men are coming to know the glory of Jesus Christ because the church has been there.

Indeed, our job is to go into those places in our society where people need to be restored; that's where you see the kingdom of God being built. When that is our witness, people can't say we're cloistered in our marble and glass cathedrals, but that we're out in the world, living the faith.

Just a Self-help Group?

The second error the world makes when it looks at the church today is seeing us as just another competitor in the free American mar-

ket of self-improvement schemes. To unbe-
lievers, we're a little bit like est or mind control or yoga—"If it makes you feel better to
put God on your side, do it."

I picked up a newspaper some time ago and
the thought for the day on the editorial page
quoted a prominent American pastor as saying:
"Put God to work for you and maximize your
potential in this divinely ordered capitalistic
system." That's not only cheap grace and bad
theology, it's heresy. God was not made for our
benefit; we were made for His pleasure. The
church does not exist to make people happy;
the church is here to make people holy.

Yet too often the message we are preaching
today is not the convicting news of sin and
salvation through none but Jesus Christ; instead, it is, "Come to God and be showered
with blessings."

Martin Luther saw things differently. He said,
"I have followed the rule not to minister com-
fort to any person except those who have become contrite and are sorrowing because of their
sin. Those who have despaired of self help."

What does the Bible tell us about our duty
as Christians? The Apostle Paul wrote to his
disciple Timothy,

All Scripture is inspired by God and profitable for teaching, for reproof, for correction, for training in righteousness; that the man of God may be adequate, equipped for every good work. I solemnly charge you in the presence of God and of Christ Jesus, who is to judge the living and the dead, and by His appearing and His kingdom: preach the Word; be ready in season and out of season; reprove, rebuke, exhort, with great patience and instruction (2 Timothy 3:16–4:2).

When I became a Christian, the first thing I did was pick up a Bible. I'm a lawyer, and my lawyer's mind demanded evidence. Is this Book really the Word of God that it claims to be, or is it a collection of legends? So I read it from cover to cover; I also read books about the Bible. I learned, for example, that the Psalms were indeed written when they said they were written. Until recent years, higher critics of Holy Scripture had claimed that the prophecy of Jesus Christ's crucifixion which is given in meticulous detail in Psalm 22 could only have been written a hundred years before His time since the torture of crucifixion hadn't even been invented at the time of David. Then the Dead Sea Scrolls confirmed what believers in an infallible, inerrant Bible have always said to be so.

I also closely examined what Jesus said about Scripture and about Himself. Go through the New Testament sometime and see how He always quoted the Old Testament as the Word of God. When Christ resisted the devil in the wilderness, three times He quoted from the Law, "It is written" (Matthew 4:4, 7, 10; cf. Deuteronomy 8:3; 6:16, 13). When He spoke to the two disciples on the road to Emmaus following His resurrection, He said,

"O foolish men and slow of heart to believe in all that the prophets have spoken! Was it not necessary for the Christ to suffer these things and to enter into His glory?" And beginning with Moses and with all the prophets, He explained to them the things concerning Himself in all the Scriptures (Luke 24:25-27).

Jesus also said, "Thy Word is truth" (John 17:17), and "not the smallest letter or stroke shall pass away from the Law, until all is accomplished" (Matthew 5:18). Beyond any question, Jesus Christ validates the Scripture.

Critics have retaliated, "How do we know that Jesus actually said the words that are in the Bible?" Well, the Hebrew custom at that time was that you never wrote down anything as true unless you had heard it with your own ears and had two eyewitnesses for corroboration. The historical evidence is that the Bible contains the actual words of Jesus.

So critics retaliate one more time. They say Jesus was mistaken when He said, "I and the Father are One" (John 10:30). Can an infallible God make a mistake? Can a holy God deceive? The attack on the authenticity of Jesus' words is really a guise for the belief that He is not who He says He is, a challenge to the fact that He was actually resurrected from the dead.

It's an attack that has gone on for nearly 2,000 years. Indeed, it began in the first century, for that is why the Apostle Paul wrote to the church at Corinth,

If Christ has not been raised, your faith is worthless; you are still in your sins. Then those also who have fallen asleep in Christ have perished. If we have hoped in Christ in this life only, we are of all men most to be pitied (1 Corinthians 15:17-19).

But if Jesus Christ was resurrected in fulfillment of the Scripture, He is who He says He is and has the authority to say that the Bible *is* the Word of God.

Oddly enough, what ultimately persuaded me of the Bible's truth was my own experience in the Watergate scandal. It was March 21, 1973, when John Dean walked into President Nixon's office and said, "Mr. President, there is a cancer growing on your presidency." And that was the day he laid out everything about the Watergate cover-up to Mr. Nixon. That's the first time we really knew it was a criminal conspiracy that could involve the White House. There was talk of perjury, obstruction of justice—the type of things that give grown men sweaty palms. It was on April 8, 1973, as John Dean confessed in his memoirs, that he went to the prosecutor to turn himself in and "to save his own skin." He would testify against the President in exchange for immunity from prosecution.

And at that point the conspiracy was gone.

Mr. Nixon didn't know it at the time, but he was finished. Jeb Magruder went to the prosecutor next; then a half-dozen other people. I took a lie detector test to show I knew nothing about the Watergate break-in. My lawyers released it to the *New York Times.* We were all scrambling to save our own skins. The Watergate cover-up, the really criminal part, lasted less than three weeks.

Put yourself in our shoes. There we were, ten or eleven of the most powerful men in the world, the colleagues of the President of the United States. We could press a button and have a jet waiting for us at Andrews Air Force Base. We could order government agencies around, deal with heads of nations. We had all this power at our fingertips, but when threatened with jail and political embarrassment, we couldn't contain a lie for even three weeks.

Now contrast Watergate with the apostles' testimony about the Resurrection. For forty years those men, who were powerless—without money, armies, or resources—proclaimed throughout Palestine and the Roman Empire that Jesus had been bodily raised from the dead. Every one of them went to jail and was persecuted. All but one died a martyr's death.

They could never have maintained their story that was so offensive to the powerful of their day unless it were true and they had seen the risen Christ. The Apostle Peter would have been just like John Dean. There would have been a deathbed confession, a smoking-gun tape, something. But the evidence is overwhelming that not once in those forty years did any of the apostles renounce Jesus. They had seen Him!

The evidence for the resurrection of Jesus Christ is more powerful than anything else we believe. By His resurrection Jesus proved He is who He says He is. Be confident in this truth. Stand on the Holy Word of God. Don't sell the world a false bill of goods. Preach the Word. Defend the faith. Live the faith.

Just a Social Club?

The third error the world makes concerning the church is seeing us as something like a Sunday morning Rotary Club, a place you join, visit to be inspired, and stay as long as you feel like staying. When people tell me, "That was a very inspiring message," I always feel disappointed because I don't want to entertain. I want to bring the truth. And the truth is convicting.

The Apostle Paul, writing to Timothy, described the church as the "pillar and support of the truth" (1 Timothy 3:15). In this context he isn't using *truth* to refer to something being factual, as in this truth: I sit at a desk that is made of wood. No, Paul is referring to *truth* in the sense that Jesus used the word when he said, "I am the truth" (John 14:6). We Christians—the church—take our stand on this revealed, propositional truth.

When he was gasping for breath, near death, Francis Schaeffer told me that the crisis we face is one of truth. "The issue is truth," he often said, "and there'll be nothing but an echo of truth left before the end of this century."

Increasingly in this age, holding this truth will make you the subject of scorn and ridicule. Increasingly Christians will be tempted to say, "I'll just edge over here a bit to be a little more in tune with the values of the society"; they'll want to join the "church as social club."

If we can't call people to be disciples and teach them to pray, to study, to live holy lives as witnesses for Jesus Christ, we have no business being a church. We might as well shut the doors and close down.

It's high time the church became bold in its witness; we have too long watered down our message for fear of offending people. The Gospel minces no words: To be a Christian is to be a member of a holy nation, the central covenant of which is that a holy God has chosen to come and live in our midst, a God who commands, "You shall be holy, for I am holy" (1 Peter 1:16). We must be a holy people, not just pious in the way we live our lives but holy in the sense that we fight for God's standards of justice and righteousness in society.

It does not matter so much what we do in this success-oriented world in which we live as what a sovereign God chooses to do through us. What really matters is not our achievements, but our right relationship with the living Lord and our willingness to live obedient Christian lives so that Christ can work through us, to be the people of hope in a world of despair. That's what Jesus means when He says, "He who has lost his life for My sake shall find it" (Matthew 10:39). The great paradox of the Christian life is that God will use you in ways you least expect. What He wants is for you to obey Him, to do as He commands.

Wherever I go, I ask people, "What is the greatest commandment of the Christian life?"

And almost every believer answers, "To love the Lord your God with all your heart, mind, and soul."

Then I follow up by asking, "What do you mean by 'love the Lord'?"

It's marvelous the kinds of answers you get when you ask that question. People generally reply, "I feel a wonderful feeling toward Him," or, "I worship Him." Yet Jesus gives us the answer in the simplest possible terms. He says, "If you love Me, you will keep My commandments" (John 14:15).

Obedience is the beginning of the Christian life; obedience is essential to truly living as a Christian. But on every side today we are beset by temptations that carry us away from God. We live in the most materialistic, egocentric time in American history. It's hard to be obedient to Christ in our pressure-packed society. It's tough to be an obedient Christian when our culture worships a false god of success. The world says, "Do your own thing"; the Gospel says, "Bear one another's burdens, and thus fulfill the Law of Christ" (Galatians 6:2). The world says, "Look out for number one"; the Gospel says to "lay down our lives for the brethren" (1 John 3:16) and to "love your neighbor as yourself" (Mark 12:31). It takes courage to be obedient, courage found only in total dependence on the Holy Spirit.

We Cannot Fail!

There isn't any hope in our society except the hope that comes from the people of God living righteously in our land. There is no ultimate hope through government or human institutions. Our brightest and best leaders are concerned with the question, "How shall we be governed?" But in the Book of Ezekiel the Jews asked: "How shall we live?" It doesn't matter who governs if society has no spiritual element to guide it.

I have seen this truth most powerfully in the area in which I've been called to spend my life: bringing Christ's healing to our crime crisis. Criminologist James Q. Wilson, among others, has tried to identify the root cause of this epidemic of violence. When he began his inquiry, he was certain that he would discover that in the great period of industrial revolution in the latter half of the nineteenth century there was a tremendous increase in crime. But, to his astonishment, he discovered a decrease. And then he looked at the years of the Great Depression. Again, there was a significant decrease in crime. Frustrated by these findings, which upset all our preconceived notions, Wilson decided to search for a single factor to correlate. The factor he found was religious faith.

When crime should have been rising in the late 1800s because of rapid urbanization, industralization, and economic dislocation, Victorian morality was sweeping across America. It was a time of intense spirituality. It was not until the conscious rejection of Victorian morality during the Roaring Twenties that crime went up. This was the era when Sigmund Freud's views were coming into vogue among "thinking" Americans: people weren't evil, just misguided or mistreated, or they required better environments. Sin was regarded as a lot of religious claptrap.

The crime rate did not decline again until the Great Depression, a time of people banding together in the face of crisis. Wilson concluded, therefore, that crime was in large part caused by a breakdown of morality. Since 1965 the violent-crime rate has steadily risen. In the same period, religious faith has waned. We have told people there are no absolutes and that they are not responsible for their own behavior. They are simply victims of a system that isn't working anymore, and they don't have to worry about it because the government is going to fix it for them. Well, the secular utopia is in reality the nightmare we see as we walk through the dark, rotten holes we call prisons all across America.

In this context, it always amazes me when I listen to politicians say, "We are going to win the war on drugs by building prisons, appointing more judges, and putting more police on the beat. I remember when President Bush announced the "War on Drugs."

Having spent seven months in prison, there wasn't one night that I did not smell marijuana burning. If you can get marijuana into a prison, with watchtowers, inspections, and prison guards, you can get it into a country. You can send the U.S. Marines to Colombia to burn all the fields, seal all the borders, and build all the prisons you want, but you won't stop drug use in this country because it isn't a problem of supply; it is a problem of demand. When there is no greater value in the lives of so many people than simply fulfilling individual desires and gratifications, then crime and drug use become inevitable. The soaring violent-crime rate is powerful testimony to the failure of the city of man, deprived of the moral influence of the City of God.

Sometimes we Christians think our ultimate power is in the ballot box, when our power is really in the cross of Jesus Christ. Realizing this, we must also realize the importance of our role as believers—faithfully to obey the holy commandments of God. We cannot allow the newspapers to define the church's role. Nor television. Nor the politicians. Man may fail, but the church—God's chosen instrument—cannot fail.

Speaking to His disciple Peter, Jesus spoke of the church of Christ: "The gates of hell shall not prevail against it" (Matthew 16:18, KJV). They never have and they never will.

Late in the last century there was a great Methodist church planter named C.C. McKay who traveled around the country planting one new church a day. While in Oregon one day, he read a newspaper report of a speech given to the Free Thinkers Society by noted lawyer and orator Robert Ingersoll. In the report Ingersoll, an atheist, was quoted as saying that the church was dying. C.C. McKay got off the train, went to the telegraph office, and cabled the following message to Robert Ingersoll:

Dear Bob,

In the Methodist church we are starting one new congregation a day. And now because of what you said, we propose to make it two.

C.C. McKay

P.S. All hail the power of Jesus' name.

The telegram prompted a series of debates between McKay and Ingersoll — most of them won by McKay — as well as a wonderful folk hymn, sung in Methodist churches all across the land.

But the most wonderful footnote of the story didn't happen until years later. In 1941 Ingersoll's grandson, Robert Ingersoll III, walked into a church in Chicago, heard the Gospel, believed, was baptized, and became a member of that congregation. So did Robert Ingersoll IV a few days afterward.

All hail the power of Jesus' name! The church is alive!

Dare to Be Different, Dare to Be Christian

Dare to Be Different, Dare to Be Christian

America is a nation in transition, in the eye of a storm that pollster Daniel Yankelovich has called a "sweeping, irreversible cultural revolution . . . transforming the rules that once guided American life." Powerful forces are shaking our very substructure.

Like all revolutions, the most profound struggle is going on in *us*. We are desperately seeking certainty in the midst of confusion and hope in the face of disillusionment. Above all, we are confounded by the maddening contradictions that plague us. Consider these few illustrations:

• The boundless affluence considered to be the fulfillment of the American dream led to indifference and spiritually destructive materialism.

• The technology that promised to lead us to a new promised land now threatens to poison it—a toxic no man's land.

• The self-fulfillment spree of the past decades led not to the expected expansion of the human potential but to isolation, loneliness, and the death of community.

Our dilemmas are compounded by a technology that dramatically telescopes history, accelerating the speed of cultural change. While it took early pioneers a full century on foot and hoof to hack their way across the wilderness of this continent, the jet age measures such distance in hours and seconds. So today's pilgrimage is that of a people being propelled through a wind tunnel, tumbling and falling helplessly, unable to gain secure footing long enough to catch their breath.

Jacques Ellul, the French lawyer-theologian, wrote:

Day after day the wind blows away the pages of our calendars, our newspapers, and our political regimes, and we glide along the stream of time without a judgment.... If we are able to live in this world ... we need to rediscover the meanings of events and the spiritual framework which our contemporaries have lost.

Precisely! We are a people wandering in a spiritual wilderness, searching frantically for our roots and crying out for an understanding of the context in which we live.

Deeper Issues

If you follow daily headlines you will quickly conclude that the dominant issues in American society are economic policy or budget deficits or social security (in every sense of the term) or conflicts between conservative and liberal political philosophies. But these are surface issues.

The deeper issues are first, what values will we live by—absolute truth, the Holy Word of God, *or* the arbitrary, relative whims of the humanist elite? And second, who will set the moral agenda—the church *or* the bureaucratic social planners and vested economic interests of secular society?

America's moral leadership is up for grabs—and that is where you and I come in. The outcome of today's revolution will be determined by how we respond to the cries of our people for moral direction and vision.

Recent government budget cutbacks put the challenge squarely before us. For fifty years politicians led us to believe that government could provide answers to all social ills. Their recipe was simple: Enact a law, add at least one government agency, pour in money, and stir continuously.

But the ever-spiraling deficit and threat of grave economic consequences shatter that myth. We are learning that there are limits to what we once thought was the endless abundance of the American economy. So government deficits must be curbed, lest the whole system grind to a halt.

But the resulting cutbacks hurt those most dependent on government aid, that is, the poor. Society's concern for its disadvantaged and oppressed is a moral issue. We Christians know from the Old Testament that a people who would sell the poor for a pair of shoes stands in fearsome judgment of Almighty God.

So the government's budget crisis raises a moral dilemma for our society and a spiritual issue for the church. How we respond will say much for the kind of people we are and hope to be; that's why I consider the budget crunch and the plight of the poor "Round Number One" in the battle for America's moral leadership.

The church faced one of its first tests in New York City several years ago, when 36,000 homeless men and women were wandering the city's streets at night. Mayor Edward Koch appealed to religious leaders for help: If each one of New York's 3,500 churches would care for just 10 homeless people, a desperate human problem could be quickly solved — and without huge government expense.

The *New York Times* reported the religious leaders' responses. One Protestant representative was concerned about protocol: "The mayor never mentioned this to me.... Nobody in his office called to apprise me of this." A Catholic spokesman sidestepped. A Jewish leader explained that many of the synagogues would not have money for increased heating bills.

The *Times* concluded: The church leaders would need more time to study the mayor's proposal. There was a disturbing silence from evangelicals.

One can almost imagine how it might sound on that day promised in Matthew 25 when our Lord says, "I was a stranger, and you did not invite Me in" (v. 43).

And the religious leaders will respond, "But, Lord, You didn't give us time to study the proposal."

I don't mean to belittle our brothers in New York; the issue is complicated and government cannot immediately transfer to the church full responsibility for the needy. But the sorry response should make us ask ourselves some tough questions. Have we become so caught up in doing our own thing, organizing vast publishing, church, and parachurch empires, that we have lost sight of our biblical mission?

Church bureaucracies can become as bogged down as government bureaucracies, so wrapped up in writing pious statements of faith, issuing press releases, and maintaining property that they forget their reason for existence: to proclaim the Good News and obey the clear commands of the Scriptures.

Of course, the Bible requires justice and righteousness from government, but it also demands that *we* care about our neighbors, clothe the naked, feed the hungry, and visit the sick and those in prison. That's *us* our Lord is talking to, and we don't discharge that obligation by paying our taxes or dropping dimes in charity boxes. We discharge it by *doing* the Word of God.

Amazing things happen when we do exercise our biblical duty. Some time ago we took six convicts, furloughed out of a federal prison in Florida, to Atlanta, where each one was assigned to stay in the home of a Prison Fellowship volunteer. Each morning the six convened for several hours of Bible study, then they converged on the homes of two widows in a deteriorating section of the city. For two weeks they insulated, weatherstripped, caulked, sealed, and painted.

It was all part of a model project demonstrating that nonviolent criminals can do something better than vegetate in a prison cell at a cost to taxpayers averaging $20,000 per year. Without red tape and delays a project valued at $21,000 was completed at no cost to the public. It also proved that people getting busy helping other people can do the job faster and cheaper than cumbersome bureaucracies.

But Atlanta also gave us lessons of far greater significance. I visited one of the widows, Roxie Vaughn, eighty-three years old and blind. When we first told Roxie her home was to be restored, she was elated. Then we told her six prisoners were going to do it, and Roxie turned ashen. You see, she had had some personal experience with crime: Her house had been broken into four times in the prior two years. She had lived in constant fear.

Well, by the third day those prisoners had worked around Roxie's home, she had them in for cookies and milk. The next afternoon television cameras caught a picture of Roxie sitting at her organ playing "Amazing Grace" with those six prisoners around her singing.

I spoke at the service at the end of the project. The widows were there. So were the volunteer families that had hosted the inmates. None of those hosts wanted to see their guests leave. The children were hugging the prisoners; the volunteers were hugging the widows. That dark, musty inner-city sanctuary that hadn't been filled in forty years was jammed full of Christians from all over Atlanta — black and white, rich and poor — in the most exciting and joyous worship imaginable. We were witnessing the incredible power of the Gospel to heal prejudices, to deliver people from fear, and to reconcile us to one another.

Our twentieth-century technology has brought clinical impersonalization: Machines solve all problems; television reduces us all to spectators as life appears in a condensed version from 6 to 7 each evening, in living color. And the by-product of modern technology is the loss of our sense of caring and awareness of one another.

Prison Fellowship recently commissioned researchers to take a comprehensive look at the underlying causes of the rampant juvenile crime sweeping the country. Though their report was substantial, it ultimately reduced the problem to one word: *alienation.* Alienation from self, family, the community, the natural environment, and God.

And the proffered solution? Stable mentors committed to working with youth one-to-one, Christians willing to stand in the gap and bridge the river of alienation that is drowning a new generation.

As we Christians get out of our pews, seek

justice, do the Word of God, and lift up Christ, we will see a sense of community restored to our land.

Think what this can mean for evangelism. The world perceives us as pious and self-centered in our protected sanctuaries and multi-million-dollar church complexes—but that is simply not where most of the sick, hurting, and hungry people are, so they never hear our message. But imagine what would happen if the poor and needy could see us where *they* live, as we meet them at their point of need.

And, if we heed that call, we will be reasserting a proud heritage of the evangelical church. In the nineteenth century, evangelicals were at the forefront of the most significant social reforms in Western society: enacting child labor laws; ending abuses in the coal mines; establishing public education and public hospitals; and abolishing slavery.

"Round Number One" in the contest for America's moral leadership is still going on; whether the church is willing and able to step up to its biblical responsibility is still to be decided. It may be the greatest question we face. For if we fail even the simple test of responding to human needs in our own community, what possible claim will we have to assume a role of genuine moral leadership in society? We dare not fail.

A Different Kingdom

We are called to live and work and serve in this world but to give our total allegiance to an entirely different kingdom, what the Apostle Peter called the "holy nation."

"You are a chosen race, a royal priesthood, a holy nation, a people for God's own possession, that you may proclaim the excellencies of Him who has called you out of darkness into His marvelous light" (1 Peter 2:9). Peter chose the very words Yahweh used in speaking to Moses on Mount Sinai, when He called His chosen people — the Jews — to be a "holy nation."

Ironic, isn't it, that Peter, the most Jewish of the disciples, the one whom God had to hit over the head three times to get him to bring the Good News to the Gentiles, the one who argued vehemently with Paul that Gentile believers must first become Jews, would be the one to use the term "holy nation," applying what had been the description of the Jews to *all* believers.

But Peter understood that the "holy nation"

was not just another description of the church, but a real nation instituted and bound together by the Holy Creator of heaven and earth, at whose sovereign pleasure all the kingdoms of man are allowed to exist. To understand that we are members of the holy nation should evoke our deepest reverence.

But we live in an age in which the church seems to be beating a steady retreat in the face of the advancing forces of secular culture.

The hard truth is that despite the much-ballyhooed religious resurgence of the seventies and eighties, Christian values are in retreat. We see this most obviously in the erosion of moral values — sexual permissiveness, the blatant parading of perversion, the continued casual disposal of unwanted unborn children, the breakup of the family, the consuming obsession with self and material acquisitions.

Or just look at crime for one example: We incarcerate more people per capita than any nation on earth, yet our murder rate is 2.6 to 8 times higher than that of other industrialized countries. A comparison of murder rates of other nations reveals that Americans between fifteen and twenty-four years of age are being killed seventy-four times more often than Austrians in that age-group and seventy-three times more often than Japanese. Murder is crime to the extreme, but statistics for property crime are abysmal. Ninety-eight percent of all Americans *will be* crime victims.

And if we are honest, we must admit there's more of the world in the church than there is the church in the world.

● A *Christianity Today* survey revealed that only 26 percent of the general public believed Jesus Christ to be fully God and fully man; among evangelicals the response climbed to only 43 percent.

● In a Gallup survey conducted for Dr. Robert Schuller, 81 percent of those polled said they considered themselves Christians. But only 42 percent knew Jesus delivered the Sermon on the Mount—and only 46 percent were able to name the four Gospels!

● Other Gallup polls revealed that in 1963, 65 percent of the American public believed the Bible to be infallible; by 1982, that number had declined to 37 percent. In 1992, 32 percent.

● In another survey, 1,382 people were asked what they considered to be the book that had most influenced them. Fifteen of them cited the Bible — barely more than 1 percent.

In 1976, when my book *Born Again* came out, I appeared on the "Today Show." Barbara Walters held up the book and said, "This is a great book." The next day a reporter asked a presidential candidate campaigning in New Hampshire, "Are you born again?" The obscure governor of Georgia answered, "Yes, I am." He won of course. It was the year of the evangelical. Being born again was fashionable.

Sixteen years later George Gallup asked Americans what institutions they most fear. The response? Fifty percent said they feared fundamentalists, while only 38 percent feared secular humanists.

We've gone from being the most fashionable group in America to being the most feared.

So it has never been more important — or, indeed, more difficult — for American Christians to understand what our citizenship in the "holy nation" means.

Eternal Citizenship

First, we must recognize that our eternal citizenship is in the kingdom of God, as clearly stated by Paul in Philippians 3:20. We are but sojourners in this nation, beloved though it is. We are clearly commanded by our Lord to seek *first* the kingdom of God (Matthew 6:33).

Many of us are frustrated by apostasy and declining morality in America today. It is evident on all sides. It's no wonder that Christians today yearn for the good ol' days of moral absolutes, when young people prayed in schools, parents retained authority over their children, folks loved their country and respected one another's property, and life was so much simpler.

Many of our brothers and sisters have decided to get involved; the most dramatic change in the American religious scene in the 1980s was the emergence of fundamentalist churches into the political arena. Notoriously separatist in the past, concerned primarily with protecting their own piety against the contaminating influences of the outside, those churches made a conscious effort to lead a Christian crusade to restore morality to America.

Indeed, the decay of American culture demands our involvement. There must be a Christian influence in every facet of society. Christians must participate, vote, work from within and without to see that government is an instrument of social justice.

But too there are grave pitfalls of failing to make clear the distinction between the holy nation and the nation-state. Christian moral and political movements, undertaken beneath the banner of simplistic God and country clichés, run this risk. Let me explain:

• First, no matter how well-motivated they are, some so-called Christian movements use God to sanctify the political prejudices of their adherents. And politicians are often willing partners in the process; I can testify from personal experience that politicians are not above using religious movements to their own advantage. The danger is that whenever we tie the Gospel to the political fortunes of any person or party, it is the Gospel that is made hostage and the Gospel that suffers.

• Second, Christian political movements can become exclusive. No one agenda can fit all moral situations.

Let us never limit God. He may burden you with one particular cause. He may burden me with another. In fact, I suspect that He assigns burdens and responsibilities throughout His kingdom; what might be on my agenda will not necessarily fit another equally dedicated Christian's agenda. The only absolute agenda is the uncompromising standard of righteousness and justice that Almighty God has woven through every page of His Holy Word.

● Third, in our passion to scrub America clean of its most obvious vices — homosexuality, abortion, pornography, etc. — we narrow the scope of Christian concern. And, by our silence, we implicitly embrace those things not on our hit list, aligning ourselves with the subtle sins of privilege, power, conspicuous affluence. We do it in a way our Lord very pointedly eschewed.

The American church, fairly or unfairly, is perceived as a white, Anglo-Saxon, upper-middle-class phenomenon. The same folks who dine at the country club on Saturday evenings, rub shoulders on padded pews at their gilded churches on Sunday mornings. The danger is that we become so identified with an affluent American lifestyle, that people who can't or won't accept the values of that culture can't or won't accept the Gospel of Christ.

Time after time I find that men and women in the prisons of America want nothing to do with the church or with Christianity. They cannot relate to our lavish buildings and stained-glass windows because they see the church as a manifestation of the culture that has rejected them and holds them prisoner.

But I see those same people come alive when I talk about Jesus the prisoner, the outcast who was followed by a dirty dozen, the One who was laid in a borrowed manger, rode on a borrowed donkey, was arrested, hung on a cross between two thieves, and then buried in a borrowed tomb. They can understand and identify with the Jesus of the Scriptures, not with a Christ who appears to have just stepped out of a Brooks Brothers catalog.

The longer I'm a Christian, the more I realize that the vague deity of American civil religion is a heretical rejection of the Christ of Holy Scripture. So don't confuse your loyalties — never assume the will of the majority and the will of God are synonymous. They may be different — and frequently are.

The Christian is committed to work for justice and righteousness, to bring the Gospel of Christ to bear in all areas of life to make a difference in society. But we do it by the integrity of our witness, not by resorting to quick, simplistic clichés.

Community

Second, as citizens of the holy nation, we necessarily and automatically become part of a community beyond ourselves. Many Christians think of conversion as personal and private. But being converted is not just being separated — or "saved" — from one's sinful past; it is being joined to a holy God and His people. That is the very essence of the covenant.

That sounds simple, but living it is not. Ours is a conspicuously egocentric era, preoccupied with our individual fulfillment and success. And I fear for the next generation — which is growing up in front of video games instead of basketball hoops or pitchers' mounds. Fifty percent of Americans watch television as they're eating dinner. So much for family conversation.

Our video and computer games are a form of electronic solitaire, as if 230 million people had so lost their capacity to relate to one another that they are more comfortable staring at twelve-inch screens shooting fake airplanes out of the air than they are looking at one another. With the prevalence of VCRs and videos, we don't even communally watch movies anymore. We prefer the couch-potato life.

We Christians must be different, prepared to live not by the self-aggrandizing rules of this culture, but by that commandment that tells us to bear one another's burdens and to lay down our lives for one another. Let me illustrate:

● Next to my conversion, the most powerful spiritual experience of my life was when, in prison, I learned that a member of my prayer group—who happened then to be the eighth-ranking Republican in the House of Representatives, now the former governor of Minnesota—had asked the President if he could serve out my remaining sentence so I could be with my wife and kids, who were experiencing serious problems. *That is citizenship in the holy nation.*

● For ten years a couple in Ohio faithfully corresponded with and periodically visited a Christian inmate who finally came up for parole. Obie hadn't been "out" in twenty years. He was sixty-one years old and apprehensive, even terrified, about the transition. How did the couple—Denny and Betty Nagy—respond? They drove across the state, picked him up at the gate, and took him to his new neighborhood—their neighborhood, where "family" could stand by for support. And there's more to the story: The Nagys hadn't stood alone in their ministry to Obie. For some years their church had paid travel and phone expenses. As Obie moved to the community, the church rallied forces to help him find employment. *That's citizenship in the holy nation.*

Since we are a part of a corporate body, we bear corporate responsibility for what happens around us. All too often we Christians act as if we secretly delight in the moral pollution around us; the more depraved the world is, the more righteous we feel by comparison.

That can be very dangerous. Remember Nehemiah: Before he undertook the extraordinary task of rebuilding the walls of Jerusalem, he prayed that God would forgive him his sins... *and the sins of his fathers* (1:6). When God's judgment comes on a people, it comes upon the just as well as the unjust.

When overworked doctors in a clinic in Chicago could not take time between abortions to fill out the forms for payment, they made hatch marks on their bloodstained smocks, casually totaling them up at the end of each day. We recoil in horror, relieved that we are not part of such a desecration of God's creation. But of course we are—inescapably so. We of the holy nation within the nation-state need to be a deeply repentant people whose hearts are contrite, whose hearts break over the practices of our culture that break the heart of God.

Worship

Third, as members of the holy nation, we worship the unseen God, who through His Son dwells in each of us. We are to respect and follow those in whom God reposes spiritual authority, but we must remember that ours is a jealous Sovereign. The first four of the Ten Commandments deal not with our sins against our fellowman but with the requirements of exclusive worship and reverence for our Creator God.

A *USA Today* poll asked people why they went to church. Forty-five percent said they went because it was good for them. "Worship" didn't even rate in the survey report. We need to rediscover the first line of an old gospel song: "I stand amazed in the presence of Jesus the Nazarene."

We Americans stand amazed in the presence

of fame for fame's sake. To be the object of adulation and worship in America, one needs only to appear frequently enough on television to be generally recognized; it has nothing to do with why the person is famous. As British journalist Henry Fairlie said,

We say correctly of some people that they idolize success, but our societies as a whole also worship it, and again the celebrity is a symbol. We do not applaud his talents, even if he should have any; we applaud his success.

Just look at the utterly idolatrous worship of Elvis Presley. A $500,000 collection of Presley artifacts toured the country some years ago, attracting as many as 200,000 viewers at each stop. The display manager, who spent $1,000 for one of the most popular items — a pair of Presley's underpants — told reporters, "I almost didn't buy them . . . but the women just went nuts over them, wanted their pictures taken with them." Millions of Americans fanatically worship the memory of this dead man who would hole up for months eating compulsively, ogling porno films, who was so stoned much of the time that he couldn't control his bowels during the night. That we have so extolled this pathetic man says more about us than Presley. As Shakespeare wrote in *Macbeth*, "Fair is foul and foul is fair." Similarly, the Bible says, "Woe to those who call evil good, and good evil" (Isaiah 5:20) and to those "whose god is their appetite, and whose glory is in their shame, who set their minds on earthly things" (Philippians 3:19). The very next verse presents the contrast: But "our citizenship is in heaven." We are to be different—daringly different.

What is it about us that causes us to withhold from God the reverence we lavish on human idols? Over and over in the White House, I met people who would fiercely complain about a policy and demand an audience with the President. But the roaring lions I escorted from the waiting room became meek lambs in the Oval Office. I saw more awe in that one room than I have seen in the sanctuaries of all our churches combined.

But that is the secular world, you say. Well, that same attitude has captured much of the Christian world. Instead of the pelvis-grinding rendition of "Hound Dog," we Christians have substituted Pepsodent smiles, sprayed-stiff hair, and syrupy baritones, all slickly directed before expensive video cameras. But just because we're electronically as good as Johnny Carson doesn't mean that we are penetrating the world with the convicting message of Christ.

The Word

Fourth, as citizens of the holy nation, we take our stand not on the shifting sands of secular relativism but on the holy and inerrant Word of God. Decisions in the world are made on the basis of expedience and changing sociological factors.

As for our government's shifting sands, I offer two opinions from the Supreme Court that show how the federal government officially views religion. The first, from 1933: "The essence of religion is belief in a relation to God involving duties superior to those arising from any human relation." I'll buy that.

But during the turmoil of the 1960s, the Court saw fit to give us a new definition of religion: "A sincere and meaningful belief which occupies in the life of its possessor a place parallel to that filled by God of those admittedly qualifying for this [conscientious] exemption."

In other words, in the eyes of the government, one certainly does not need God to be religious; if one is occupied by a sincere and meaningful belief in a tuna fish, perhaps, that will do just fine.

But as citizens of the kingdom of God, we stand on the unchanging, immutable Word of God. Without it, we Christians have nothing.

Taking our stand on biblical truth can be our only defense against our culture's penchant to reduce all issues to simplistic suppositions and glib answers. We impatiently expect to get solutions to the most profound ambiguities of life the same way we drive up to the fast-food counter: one double burger, chocolate shake, and an order of fries. We are faddists. Just look at the rash of new diets and instant physical-conditioning courses that week after week dominate our bestseller lists.

The problem is, that "easy-answer" mentality is invading the Christian church: We want scorecards by which we can instantly rate our politicians, new catch acronyms for salvation, time-saving techniques for discipleship. But formulas don't convert people; slick slogans and cute phrases are no substitute for hard spiritual truth.

In our well-intentioned effort to reach unsaved masses, we often make the Gospel message itself sound easy, unthreatening, a painless answer to all life's ills. We portray a loving God who forgives all and asks nothing in return. Now, that may tickle the ears of this pleasure-seeking generation, but it is nothing less than heresy.

As citizens in the holy nation, we must challenge presuppositions — not only of society as a whole but of the evangelical subculture as well. The Gospel of Jesus Christ must be the bad news of the conviction of sin before it can be the Good News of redemption.

Some years ago I was with Billy Graham who admonished me to follow his example in this regard: Every time he preaches he reads one particular verse, "For all have sinned and fall short of the glory of God" (Romans 3:23).

On "60 Minutes" Mike Wallace once interviewed a survivor of Auschwitz, a key witness against Adolf Eichmann, the mastermind of the Holocaust. Upon entering the courtroom and facing Eichmann, this witness began to tremble. Weeping uncontrollably, he collapsed.

When Mike Wallace asked this man why he had collapsed—was it reliving the memories, the nightmares, and the griefs?—the man answered: "No. I collapsed because I was afraid about myself. I saw that I am exactly like him, capable of this."

Now I've been interviewed by Mike Wallace and he's a pro. It's hard to shake him, but this answer did. He almost couldn't ask the next question. He stared at the man, then turned to the camera and said, "That poses a question. Was Eichmann a monster, a mad man, or something even more terrifying? Was he normal?"

All have sinned. The Word of God proclaims it and the Word of God stands, despite the prevalent myth of the twentieth century—that man is by nature good.

In 1981 a very readable little book was published with the appealing title *When Bad Things Happen to Good People*. Written by a Boston rabbi, Harold Kushner, it was an overnight sensation, fifty-two weeks on the *New York Times* bestseller list, millions of copies sold. The title of the book implies that if things go "wrong," it can't be our own fault. There has to be an explanation. What can it be?

Kushner's thesis is simple enough: God is all-loving but not all-powerful; the bad things that happen to us are out of His control. So the rabbi exhorts his readers to "learn to love and forgive Him [God] despite His limitations."

Now it will be immediately obvious to you that this god of Kushner's is not the God of Abraham and of Israel, not the all-powerful God revealed in the Scriptures.

But you may say, so what? If one rabbi rejects Jewish orthodoxy and writes a book offering easy answers to life's great mysteries and a hungry and hurting people gobble it up, what's the surprise?

Well, if that were the whole story, you'd be right. But there's more.

The book jacket carried the ringing endorsements of one of America's leading Christian personalities, as well as a seminary professor. It was widely distributed in Christian churches; in fact, I finally decided to read it only after a dozen or more evangelicals recommended it to me. Pastors preached from it. It was a big seller in many Christian bookstores.

When I looked around for critical comment I found only a few Christian publications negatively reviewing the book; others were silent.

Even Rabbi Kushner said he was surprised his book had not received more criticism. When I wrote a critical article about the book for Prison Fellowship's *Jubilee* newsletter, I was deluged with mail, most of it saying, "Amen, someone's finally speaking out." But several pastors angrily denounced me for challenging a book they had found "comforting to their congregations."

"Comforting?" Indeed. So might doses of narcotics be comforting.

Kushner's book wasn't just the skewed theology of one rabbi; it was — and is — a national phenomenon, one of the most significant books in several years, enormously influencing our culture's perception of God. And we Christians went right along with the game, embracing it, even promoting it. My friends, that is not just buying into the errors of the secular culture; it is not a slight compromise with so-called realism. It is treachery to God; it is changing sides in the battle; it is promoting blasphemy. It is throwing aside the Word of God rather than standing on it as our authority.

And Kushner's book is not, I'm sorry to say, the only example. Whatever is hot in America's pop culture finds its way into the Christian market dressed in evangelical jargon. Many Christian "how-to" books, records, and tapes simply tell us how to use God as a lever to get whatever it is we desire. Get thin. Get successful. Get rich. Such religious adaptions of the self-indulgent, egocentric, materialistic culture are not only Jesus-justified hedonism but dreadful heresy — for they suggest that the majestic Creator God of this universe exists for man's pleasure rather than vice versa.

So it is that we have, I fear, slipped unknowingly into a state of moral paralysis. We are so comfortable with the "comforting" world's ways that we no longer are able to discern what is false and what is true. We have forgotten that moral confusion is the enemy's favorite weapon.

For Satan comes not in a red suit carrying a pitchfork; rather, as Shakespeare wrote in *King Lear*, the devil is a gentleman. Before his fall he was called Lucifer, the angel of light and knowledge; in the Garden of Eden, he was the most attractive of all the animals. And today he cloaks his propaganda in the conventional wisdom of the times — the rights of men and women to pursue the pleasure principle first articulated by John Stuart Mill. The pursuit of happiness, immediate and temporal, has become a moral obligation.

And the deceiver uses the bludgeon sparingly, preferring little subtleties, inferences, and suggestions which slip through the lines of Christian defenses, then over time establish themselves as legitimate. It's an insidious process of gradual compromise that has nothing to do with living as a citizen of heaven, in disciplined submission to the Word of God.

We must point people to the Holy Bible in their search for truth and answers. We who follow Christ must take our stand the only place we can—on the holy, infallible Word of God. We don't have anything else.

I use the word "infallible" advisedly. There is no issue I've wrestled with harder since I've been a Christian than my view of the Scriptures. My lawyer's mind demanded evidence before I could believe the Bible to be without error. But the more I probed, the clearer that truth became. Ironically, it was as a result of my Watergate experiences that I became utterly convinced that the Bible is absolutely authoritative—God's inerrant revelation. Life can be lived only in absolute and disciplined submission to its authority.

Righteous Living

Fifth, we are commanded to seek first not only the kingdom of God—don't stop there—but His righteousness as well.

Righteousness or holy living is often seen by Christians as maintaining chaste sexual standards, tithing, faithful church attendance, being friendly to those around us. Well, those are indeed Christian responsibilities, but only the beginning of holy living.

And many believers categorize their refraining from alcohol, tobacco, cards, and dancing as holy living. Though God may call you to that type of witness, it is only skimming the surface at best. That is piety. And we must never, never confuse piety with righteousness.

Righteousness was defined by Yahweh at Mount Sinai and interpreted by the fiery words of His prophets from Isaiah to Amos to Habakkuk and, ultimately, by the life of His Son, Jesus. God's definition of righteousness is based on justice for all people, especially the unfortunate: You shall not sell the poor for a pair of shoes, nor take away the coat of a man who borrows from you; you shall pay your em-

ployees a just wage; you shall care for widows
and orphans; you shall hate evil and do good.
"Remodel your courts into true halls of justice," thundered the Prophet Amos (see Amos
5:15). "Let justice roll down like waters and
righteousness like an ever-flowing stream" (v.
24). That's God's standard of righteousness
and holy living.

After ten years in a Soviet gulag, Alexander
Solzhenitsyn wrote, "Bless you, prison, for
having been in my life." For it was there he
learned that "the meaning of earthly existence
lies, not as we have grown used to thinking, in
prospering, but in the development of the
soul." I too can say, "Bless you prison," for it
was there that I learned to see justice in the
way that Amos and Micah and Jeremiah and
Isaiah saw it, the way it is to be in the holy
nation.

When I was in law and politics, I believed
justice was determined by a majority vote, 50
percent plus one. Justice was simply the law,
which I tried to influence, often on behalf of
very affluent clients. In the White House I saw
justice as the sum of rules and policies that I
tried to shape, often on behalf of those people
whose influence — or campaign contribution —

was significant enough to get them past the White House gates and into my office.

Then too I had grown up in the insecurity of the Depression, believing deeply in the work ethic; justice was also protecting individual's earnings and keeping the government from interfering with their rights.

Finally, of course, justice was the instrument for punishing and removing from society those who refused — or were unable — to live by the rules that people like myself made.

But from a prison cell I saw men condemned to waste away for long years — for what seemed like trivial offenses. Like most people, I had thought prisons were populated by violent, dangerous criminals. What a shock to find that the man in the bunk next to me was a former bank vice-president who battled the government for nine years over $3,000 of tax evasion. For a first offense, he received a three-year sentence. I found young men who couldn't afford lawyers. I found others who were sentenced without knowing why — or for how long. It was in a prison cell that I came to understand why God makes special demands on His people to care for the oppressed, sick, suffering, and needy.

Justice is not achieved in God's eyes until a society is as concerned with the rights and dignity of the person in a prison cell as it is with the one in the executive suite.

If we're honest, I suspect we will agree that we're as far away from that standard today as the holy nation was in the time of Amos. But that standard is what you and I must work for.

Obedience

Sixth, we must be prepared as citizens of the holy nation to take our stand in faithful obedience to our Lord, to make a difference with our lives. That will probably mean standing against the culture in "a bold and majestic witness to the holy commandments of God," as Carl Henry has put it. That does not just mean contributing or paying dues to some moralistic crusade. It means standing in the gap, if need be, by yourself.

The late Francis Schaeffer once wrote and told me of meeting believers in various walks of life whose Christian faith was making absolutely no difference in their vocations. He concluded,

We talk a lot about the need of having true Christians getting into the media, the chaplaincy, etc. . . . but there is no use for our people getting into the media or the chaplaincy or anything else unless they are willing for confrontation when necessary, even when it is costly to their careers.

Exactly right. Let me give you one illustration — there are many — of what it can mean for a Christian to take his stand against the culture.

In 1977 Harry Fred Palmer, a Vietnam veteran, was arrested in Elkhart, Indiana for burglary; while in jail awaiting trial he accepted Christ. His offense carried a mandatory minimum sentence of ten years — although that law, acknowledged as arbitrary by the legislature, had been changed eighteen days after Palmer's arrest.

The judge assigned to the case, William Bontrager, had himself been converted to Christ recently. He reviewed the facts, concluded the ten-year minimum statute unconstitutional, and sentenced Palmer to one year in prison with the provision he thereafter make restitution to those he had robbed, and perform community service.

Palmer did just that. He served his year, a model prisoner, active in Prison Fellowship programs. After his release he began paying back his victims and was reunited with his wife and family. The case was a model of justice, restitution, and restoration.

But the Indiana Supreme Court swung into action, claiming that Bontrager's suspension of the mandatory sentence was unconstitutional. Palmer should serve the remaining nine years of his automatic sentence, they said, even though the law requiring it was no longer in existence. They ordered Bontrager to send him back to jail.

For Bontrager, the court's order was clearly a case of choosing to obey the law of man or the law of God. He had been reading the Old Testament prophets; God's demands for justice and righteousness had seared his conscience. He knew the Supreme Court's order would serve neither, merely a technicality of the law.

So he disqualified himself, turning the case over to another judge. A nightmarish sequence of events followed. The court slammed Palmer back behind bars, declared Bontrager in contempt, fined him $500, and sentenced him to thirty days in prison. Though that sentence was suspended, the court began proceedings to remove him from the bench. Rather than allow his own struggle to endanger Palmer's chance for appeals, Judge Bontrager resigned.

It was not a painless decision. He gave up a comfortable salary, the judgeship he had worked all his life to attain, and the security of community respect. But Judge Bontrager's spiritual discernment was keen—he knew to send a man back to prison for a debt he had already paid was at odds with the standard of justice of the holy God he served. So he had to take his stand—whatever the cost.

Though your arena may not be the courtroom, I guarantee you will have many opportunities, small and large, to take your stand. If not, you need to question your own commitment. Conformity is the high priest of American culture and has infiltrated the holy nation.

We live in an age in which compromise is applauded as one of the highest virtues of civilized men. Our pluralistic form of government uses compromise to make an issue acceptable to the greatest number of people by a process of negotiation.

But what may occasionally work in the secular world is not necessarily God's wisdom. A compromise of hot and cold yields lukewarm. And God, speaking in Revelation, is resolute about lukewarmness: "I know your deeds, that you are neither cold nor hot.... So because you are lukewarm, and neither hot nor cold, I will spit you out of My mouth" (3:15-16).

It is not easy, but, I beseech you, *dare to be different.* Dare to live as a citizen of the holy nation.

Time for Action

Seventh, and finally, citizens of the holy nation must participate in the human drama. Much of the church today has withdrawn, seeking refuge on the high ground. Our multi-million-dollar church complexes surrounded by acres of paved parking lots are as remote and protected as walled medieval fortresses, protected from the swirling waters where most of the sick, hungry, and hurting people are. So those in need cannot identify with us and will consequently never hear our message. But imagine what would happen if they see us where they live, as we met them at their point of need.

Jacques Ellul wrote that until we have

really understood the actual plight of our contemporaries and we have heard their cry of anguish, until we have shared their suffering both physical and spiritual, and their despair and desolation, then we shall be able to proclaim the Word of God, but not until then.

The Apostle Paul called it the fellowship of suffering (Philippians 3:10). It is a spiritual mystery—suffering with others draws us closer to our Christ who suffered for us. Being in prison has given me this insight. For the most meaningful communions I have had with my Lord have not been in the great cathedrals of the world I've been privileged to preach in nor in the parliaments where I have spoken nor in the most influential gatherings of Christian leaders. They have been instead on my knees on the grimy, concrete floor of a rotten prison cell with my hand on the shoulder of a tough convict who sobs with joy as we meet Another who was in prison, executed, and rose from a tomb for us—His name is Jesus.

My friends, take your posts. You have been called out by the most high and holy God to serve Him in the building of His holy nation.

You are called not to be successful or to meet any of the other counterfeit standards of this world, but to be faithful and to be expended in the cause of serving the risen and returning Christ.